How to Edit a Book

With a Friend

Dorothy May Mercer

How to For You Series #12

© 2014 Mercer Publications & Ministries, Inc.

www.MercerPublications.com

© 2015 Mercer Publications & Ministries, Inc.

Stanwood, Michigan, USA

All rights reserved.

ISBN 13: 978-1-62329-037-5
ISBN 10: 1-62329-037-6

Mercer Publications & Ministries, Inc.
Stanwood, Michigan, USA

Very informative for the self-published author, October 15, 2014

By

MegaReader (East Anglia, UK) - See all my reviews

This review is from: **How to Edit a Book: With a Friend (How To For You Book 12) (Kindle Edition)**

"Very informative and helpful. I will definitely be referring to this book when I edit my latest novel. There's a wealth of information here for the self-published author."

TABLE OF CONTENTS

Introduction 5

Chapter 1 Instructions for the Editor 7

  Advanced 10

  Original showing Markup 11

Chapter 2 Send Your Changes to Author 13

Chapter 3 Author's Instructions 15

  Advanced 16

Chapter 4 Further Editing 19

  More Advanced 19

Introduction

Here's a question for you. What is the second piece of advice indie-publishers receive, right after "Get a professional cover?"

If you answered, "Hire a professional editor," you would be right. Of course, after you drop $xxx.00 for the cover, you may need to spend more than twice that for an editor. Really? *On second thought, maybe a do-it-yourself edit will suffice.* (Actually, it probably will not.)

What to do? How about asking a good friend to do it for free? If you have friends like that, all I can say is "Lucky you." A more likely scenario is a swap—yes a swap. If you can find a skilled indie author, willing to swap editing services, this article is for you.

But, you say, I cannot edit. Okay, what skills do you have? You are a writer, are you not? Well then, you can proofread, buy books, post on Twitter, Pinterest and Facebook, "like" a blog, and post reviews. Choose a successful author and I promise you, he/she will need your services.

Microsoft Word has made it so much easier for two or more people to do an edit. Gone are the old days when geeks with Masters degrees in English grammar scrutinized stacks of typed manuscripts, scribbling mysterious notes in margins and between double spaced lines, utilizing a collection of colored pens and pencils. Now, everything is digital and so easy.

It is necessary, however, to understand a few commands. We will use the "Review" command in Microsoft Word 2007 and above. This booklet will take you through the commands, step by step. We will begin with instructions for the Editor and continue with instructions for the Author. Before long you, too, will carry the exalted credit line "editor."

Chapter 1 Instructions for the Editor

For the purposes of this book, we will assume that you know the basics of English grammar, proper sentence and paragraph construction, as well as the rudiments of good writing. Before you begin editing, or writing for that matter, it is good to brush up on these techniques and equip yourself with a minimum of two good reference books, an English grammar and a dictionary. Your Word program has both, but, while useful, they are not always correct or detailed enough for this purpose.

You have agreed to edit a friend's book in exchange for a suitable swap. Allow about one week's work for the first edit, plus extra part-time work for re-editing and final editing.

Ask your author friend to proofread his/her book at least once, twice is better. Also, have her go through the markings made by Microsoft Word, correcting as needed. The more perfect the document, the easier will be your task.

We are choosing to use Microsoft Word 2007 or above. It is possible that you can adapt these instructions to other software, but you and your author should be working with the same basic software.

Have your author email you a .doc or .docx of his book, as an attachment. (There are other ways to send the book back and forth, but that is another article. For now, email works just fine.)

For the purposes of this article we will name the book, "My First Book." Open the attachment, using Microsoft Word, and save it in a special folder on your computer. (I like to store this folder under "My Documents" with a shortcut to my desktop.) Next, save it in the same place, again, "Save As" with a new name, "My First Book 1." As you and your author work on this document, each new version will have a new number, "My First Book 2," "My First Book 3" and so on. Otherwise, it is very easy to lose track of which version you have open. Now, you are ready to begin work on "My First Book 1."

Go to the special folder and open "My First Book 1."

Your first task will be to ascertain whether Author has formatted the book correctly. Let's hope that this is the case. (If not, refer to my booklets, *"How to Better Format a Paragraph,"* and *"How to Format Your Book for Printing."*) Make any final corrections to the formatting and save as "My First Book 2." Email this version to Author for approval.

Assuming Author is happy with your formatting, open version 2 on your desktop. Save as "My First Book 3" In the "Home" toolbar, open "Review."

Click "Track Changes."

Start reading the book, from the very beginning, paying attention to every single word of the credits, footnotes and headings. Continue reading, word by word, until you encounter something that needs to be changed. This could be as simple as a typo, comma, quotation, capitalization, or an italicized or misspelled word etc., or it could be a big change such as deleting or rewording a sentence, paragraph or entire scene. In either case, make the changes, as follows:

Highlight and/or delete the error in the same way you would with any document, and type in the change(s). The program will draw a line through your deletes, save, and track all your changes in red.

From time to time you will need to add a comment, either to explain your change, make suggestions or add a word of praise and encouragement. While in the "Review" toolbar, click "New Comment." A balloon will open. Type your comment in the balloon.

Note: You have a choice of placing your balloons off to the side, or in line with the text. See those options under "Balloons."

Note: Also, note that in the "Comments" section you have three commands, "Delete," "Previous" and "Next." These commands are handy whenever you need to delete or edit a comment."

To continue reading simply click back in the body of the text.

From time to time, you may need to delete a correction that you have previously made. Sometimes the regular "delete" command merely messes you up. Learn to use the curlicue back arrow (found in the extreme upper left of your window) to reverse your most recent key strokes one by one.

Occasionally, you may want to make a correction in the document that you do not wish to record. An example might be where the author left out a space. You think, *There is no need to bother having the author okay this obvious change*. In this case, you decide to make the correction without tracking the change. Before you make the change, click "Track Changes." This toggles the tracking device to "off." Go ahead and fix the space, or make any correction, and click "Track Changes" again to turn it on. Continue reading and editing.

From time to time, remember to click "Save." Forget this at your peril, God forbid.

Advanced

After you have become familiar with the program, you may experiment with the three commands in the "Tracking" section, as follows:

Original Showing Markup

Show Markup

Reviewing Pane

Go ahead and click on them one by one. We think they are self-explanatory. If they make sense to you, you may skip the following remarks.

Original Showing Markup

This is handy for you when you want to see how the document looked before you started, or how it will look after your changes have been made. You can toggle at will among four choices, Original, Original Showing [Your] Markups, Final Showing [All] Markups, and Final. Whenever you have made a bunch of changes you may want to see what it will look like in its final form. Simply click Final. You can go back to editing by clicking Original Showing Markup. Make sure that Track Changes is toggled on.

While you are looking around, click Show Markup. Notice the various options that are "on." Pull down Reviewers. Notice your name on the list.

Finally, check out Reviewing Pane. All your reviews will appear on a list, with a summary at the top. You have a choice of horizontal or vertical. Click x to close this window. Continue editing by clicking Original Showing Markup. Make sure that Track Changes is toggled on.

My Notes:

Chapter 2 Send Your Changes to Author

You may have reason to send your changes one or more chapters at a time. We understand. But, bear in mind that it can become tricky trying to keep track of the versions. This is especially true if this is your author's first experience. If you choose to do this, I recommend that you stop editing on Version 3 and wait until Author sends you back Version 4 before you continue editing.

Let's assume that you complete editing the entire book before you send it to Author. Now, it is a simple matter to Save this version, attach it to an email and send it off. The next step it up to the author.

My Notes:

Chapter 3 Author's Instructions

The long anticipated day has arrived. Your edited manuscript has arrived in the morning's email. Now your job begins.

First, save this document, using Microsoft Word, in your special folder.

Next, using "Save As," save the document again, assigning a new name, "My First Book 3." (Substitute *your book's name* 3). (Choose a new number.) You will work with this version now. Each time you make changes you will save the new version with the next number in the sequence, version 3, 4, 5, and so on.

Hint: We recommend that you delete the old versions, from time to time, just to keep things neat and tidy. Also, it prevents any confusion over which version is up now. These old versions will remain available in your trash can indefinitely, until you carry out the trash.

On the toolbar, click "Review." Notice the section marked Changes. You will use this section to go through Editor's changes, one by one, utilizing the two commands, Accept, Reject. You may use the remaining two commands, Previous and Next, for navigation.

Click next and the program will take you to the first change. Look it over and decide whether to accept or reject. Click on a choice. The program will jump to the next change. Continue accepting or rejecting through until the end. Remember to save, from time to time.

Read the comments as you encounter them. To delete, click in the comment. Use "delete comment" command in the toolbar.

If you change your mind, you can use "previous" to click back through the changes. Another handy gadget is the curlicue (undo) arrow in the upper left corner of your screen. This will reverse your previous key strokes one by one with each click. You can go forward and back using these arrows.

You can make further changes, yourself, as you go. The program will track your changes, so long as you keep the "Track Changes" switch on. See "Advanced."

Advanced

On the Review toolbar, click "Track Changes." Pull down "Show Markup" and click "Reviewers." Your computer's name should be added to the list.

Now, you can proceed through your document making and tracking your changes. (See Editing Instructions above.) You may also add comments. Simply click in the body where you wish to comment and click the "new comment" button in the review toolbar. Save this new version with a new number. Send it to your Editor as an email attachment.

My Notes:

Chapter 4 Further Editing

The document can be sent back and forth between the two of you until you are pleased with the results. Remember to save each new version with a new number and store the old versions in your trash can.

When finished, keep the Final and send all the previous versions to the trash can. You are now ready to prepare it for publishing in whatever form you choose, Print version, and any of the available Ebook venues. Give each version a suitable name, defining its purpose.

More Advanced

It is quite possible to do group editing with two or more editors, plus the author. Each new editor tracks changes under their name. When the new editor opens "Review/Track Changes," the program will automatically recognize this person's computer and will enter the new name on the list of names under "Review/Show Markup/Reviewers." That new reviewer's changes and comments will be defined by the new name and a new color. Now, when the Reviewing Pane is opened, each revision will be identified by name.

Thank You !

The Complete *How to For You* Series:

By Dorothy May Mercer

1. How to Write Sentences and Paragraphs *in Your Novel*
2. How to Install a Link in Your Document
3. How to Sell Your eBook Using Amazon Free Days
4. How to Prepare Your Book for Kindle
5. How to Fix Errors in Your Document, *Find and Replace Globally*
6. How to Use Your Book for Free Ads
7. How to Design and Format Your Paragraphs
8. How to Design a Kindle eBook Cover
9. How to Install Your Kindle Cover on Createspace, *and Vice Versa*
10. How to Add an Interactive Table of Contents
11. How to Format Your Book, for Publishing *Two Editions, Ebook and Print*
12. How to Edit a Book, *With a Friend, Two Editions, Ebook and Print*
13. How to Write Great Dialog *Two Editions, Ebook and Print*

14. How to Market Your Book, *Marketing 101–Two Editions, Ebook and Print*
15. Cover Designing Bargain Bundle,-Two For One
16. Marketing Bargain Bundle, Two For One
17. Marketing Bargain Bundle, Three For One
18. Formatting Bargain Bundle, Two For One
19. Coming soon: "Now That You're On Your Way, What Next?" "Marketing 201"

For prices and ordering information please go to one of these web sites:

www.MercerPublications.com

www.Amazon.com/DorothyMayMercer

More Entertaining books from Mercer Publications, Inc.

In business since 1993

by Dorothy May Mercer and other distinguished authors:

The McBride Series novels
Available-- Ebook and Print formats.

Starring Det. Lt. Mike McBride

The McBride Series:
"Car 006 Responding"
"The Cocaine Chase"
"The Golden Coin"
"The Cartel Wars"
"The Gang Bust"

The Washington McBride Series
"The Fairfax Fix"
Starring Senator Mike McBride

"The Arlington Alias"
"The Savage Surrogate"
Starring wife Juliette McBride, investigative reporter
and Lady Dog, famous Seal-trained tracking and service dog.

The New McBride Romances, Series
"Fran and Max" the Bungalow
Coming in 2015, "Cynthia and Dan"

GO HERE TO ORDER THIS AND PREVIEW OTHER EXCITING AND ENTERTAINING NOVELS:

http://www.MercerPublications.com

Historical books by Dorothy May Mercer:

"Leon and Esther," an historical Christian love story.

"Stories I Haven't Told," an autobiography

Travel Books With Colored Photographs:

By Dorothy May Mercer and Photographer Dave Mercer

"Africa and Back" With Dave and Dorothy,

A travel journal with color photographs.

Hawaii and Back, Vol.1, Kauai, With Dave and Dorothy

A travel journal with color photographs.

Hawaii and Back, Vol 2, Maui, With Dave and Dorothy

A travel journal with color photographs.

Hawaii and Back, Vol 3, Oahu, With Dave and Dorothy

A travel journal with color photographs.

Coming in 2015 Hawaii and Back, Vol 4, The Big Island, With Dave and Dorothy

<u>More Books edited and published by Mercer Publications & Ministries, Inc.:</u>

~Recommended~

"Sensual Bond" Five-Part Romantic Saga, by Netty Ejike

"Stormy Affair," Romance by Netty Ejike

"He Called Her Hat," That Tough Little Lady, by Myron C. McDonald

"Notes From John," by Marcia McMahon

Ascension Teaching with Archangel Michael, by Marcia McMahon

"Remember How Much I Love You," by Dale L. Williams, M.D.

"The Inheritance From Hell," by R.D. Margot

www.ingramcontent.com/pod-product-compliance
Lightning Source LLC
Chambersburg PA
CBHW061317040426
42444CB00010B/2681